THE COMPLETE BOOK OF THE NIGHT

Sally Tagholm

NEW YORK

Editor   Hannah Wilson
Coordinating editor   Terry Moore
Designer   Jane Buckley
Production   Caroline Hansell
DTP manager   Nicky Studdart
DTP coordinator   Primrose Burton
Picture research manager   Jane Lambert
Picture research   Juliet Duff and Audrey Reynolds

The publisher would like to thank the following illustrators:
Andrea Brun (Luigi Galante), Julian Baker, Julian Baum, Peter Dennis
(Linda Rogers Associates), Ceri Llewellyn, Ray Grinaway, Keith Hume, Josephine Martin,
David Rushby, Roger Stewart (Kevin Jones Associates) and Gareth Williams

The publisher would also like to thank the following people:
Valerie Barclay, Julie Ferris, Jennie Morris, Dr. Phill Read, Jane Tassie, and Ben Wilson

The publisher would also like to thank the following for supplying photographs:
Mountain Camera Picture Library/John Cleare: 8cl; The Bridgeman Art Library/The Victoria
& Albert Museum: 9tl; Science Photo Library/NASA: 9cr; Art Directors & Trip Photographic
Library/H Rogers: 12tl; Science Photo Library/James Holmes/Janssen Pharmaceutical Ltd: 13br;
The Stock Market/Pete Saloutos: 23br; gettyone/Stone/Glen Allison: 24bl; Science Photo Library/
Klaus Guldbrandsen: 25tl; The Art Archive: 27tr; Corbis: 31cr, 37tr; gettyone/Stone/Mike
McQueen: 40tl; Robert Harding Picture Library/L Taylor: 41tr; Collections/Brian Shuel: 41cr;
NHPA/Eric Soder: 44tl; Science Photo Library/George Post: 44bl; Bruce Coleman Collection/
Kim Taylor: 49cr, br; gettyone/Stone/Chad Slattery: 64cl; The Aviation Picture Library: 65cr;
Science Photo Library: 71br, 90br, 91tr; Corbis: 82–83; NASA: 88tl, cl, bl, 89tr, cr, br
Every effort has been made to trace the copyright holders of the photographs.
The publisher apologizes for any inconvenience caused.

KINGFISHER
Larousse Kingfisher Chambers Inc.
80 Maiden Lane
New York, New York 10038
www.kingfisherpub.com

First published in 2001
2 4 6 8 10 9 7 5 3 1

1TR/0501/TWP/CLSN/150SMA

LIBRARY OF CONGRESS CATALOGING-IN-PUBLICATION DATA
Tagholm, Sally.
The complete book of the night / by Sally Tagholm.—1st ed.
p. cm.
Includes index.
ISBN 0-7534-5323-1
1. Night—Juvenile literature. [1. Night.] I. Title.

QB633 . T34 2001
525'—dc21   2001018661

Printed in Singapore

CONTENTS

NIGHT FALLS

As the sun sinks below the horizon, draining the earth of its warmth and light, the moon waits quietly in the sky, ready to cast its pale glow into the darkness. For many it is the end of the day, a time to sleep; for others, it is just the beginning. . . .

BEDTIME

As darkness falls it is time to brush your teeth and get ready for bed. Bedtime always seems to come too soon, but there is nothing like being tucked into your own bed and drifting off to sleep. But what happens when we sleep? Where and why do we sleep? What are dreams? Bedtime is an adventure we have every night without really knowing much about it.

Beds

Beds come in all kinds of shapes and sizes—
from tiny cribs for babies to king-size, four-
poster beds for those who like a little luxury.
If you are on the move, you need to carry a light,
practical bed that fits in with your adventures.

Whatever type of bed you have, make sure it is
comfortable—your body needs a good rest every
night. Firm beds are the best because they give your back
good support while you sleep. Don't forget that beds can be
fun, too—there are bunk beds, water beds, sofa beds, and
even beds shaped like cars or spaceships! King Louis XIV
of France loved staying in bed so much that he often held
court there. He had a collection of 413 different beds!

Mountaineers often spend the night halfway
up snowy mountains. Their beds are portable
ledges, or portaledges, which they secure to
the rock face. The ledges are just big enough
to sleep on when you are tucked inside a
sleeping bag. The climbers sleep wearing
harnesses attached separately to the rock,
so that if the ledges fall from the mountain
in the night, the climbers will not!

In the past mattresses were stuffed with straw or feathers and did not have any springs. The bases of beds were often crisscrossed ropes, which were tightened regularly to stop them from sagging—this explains the expression "sleep tight." In cool climates people once slept under thick blankets and wore nightcaps to keep warm. Today heating, electric blankets, and cozy comforters keep out the cold at night.

The Great Bed of Ware is a huge, elaborately carved, four-poster bed built at the end of the 1500s in England. It first stood in the town of Ware in an inn, possibly as a tourist attraction because of its enormous size. The story goes that it once slept 68 people at one time!

Ancient Egyptians slept on narrow, wooden beds, and instead of pillows, they used small neck rests. In Japan many people sleep on futons—mattresses that are stored in cupboards during the day and rolled out onto tatami mats at night. Jungle explorers prefer hammocks because they can be hung between trees above muddy ground and away from curious animals. Mosquito nets soaked in insect repellent ward off unwelcome bugs.

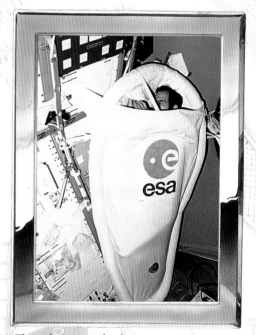

There is no gravity in space, so astronauts sleep in tethered sleeping bags that do not float away. These beds can point in any direction—even upright—because there is no up or down in space. Sleep is scheduled—there is no day or night in space either. Sometimes the mission control center on Earth plays music to wake the astronauts!

Brushing Your teeth

Roman emperors used to have special slaves to clean their teeth for them, but you probably don't—so remember to brush your teeth before you go to bed!

Germs can build up around your teeth and gums, causing tooth decay and bad breath, so you have to brush your teeth thoroughly for about two minutes in the morning and before you go to bed at night.

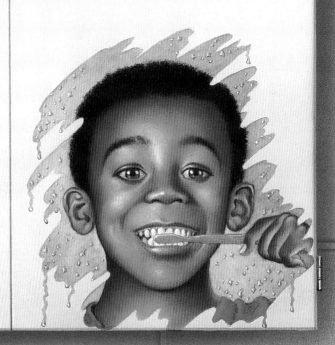

In the past people used small sticks to clean their teeth. Today we use toothbrushes—even hightech electric ones. We also use modern toothpastes that contain fluoride. Long ago strange pastes and powders were used. They contained all kinds of ingredients—like eggshells and dried flowers! It has always been a good idea to spit out toothpaste!

When one of your baby teeth falls out, don't forget to hide it under your pillow before you go to bed. Some people think that the tooth fairy will come to take it in the middle of the night. If you are lucky, she may leave some money under your pillow.

The ancient Egyptians treated a toothache by pressing warm, dead mice against their cheeks over the painful spot—a treatment not recommended today! If you have a toothache, go to your dentist and try to cut down on sugary snacks and drinks, which can cause the problem.

When it is really hot, crocodiles wallow in the water and open their mouths wide to cool themselves down. Sometimes birds perch inside their mouths and hop around, pecking out insects and pieces of food that are stuck in their teeth—just like living toothpicks!

Sleeping

Most of us spend about a third of our lives asleep, recharging our batteries for the next day. Sleep is so important that we can survive longer without food than we can without sleep. It is no wonder Napoleon I, the French general and emperor, failed when he tried not to sleep at all!

When we sleep, our pulse rate and blood pressure drop, and our breathing slows. This gives our body and brain a chance to rest. Growth hormones are released in children when they sleep, so sleep helps them to grow. Sleep also helps the proteins in our cells that keep us looking healthy. Sleep really is "beauty sleep"!

When some people are anxious or overtired, they walk or talk in their sleep. Others grind their teeth, and many people are loud snorers. But because we often experience amnesia, or forgetfulness, after sleep, it is difficult to know exactly what happens when we sleep.

Different animals need different amounts of sleep—the giant armadillo, one of the laziest animals around, needs about 18 hours at a time, but giraffes sleep for only two hours. The brains of bottle-nosed dolphins are divided into halves that take turns to sleep. This means that the dolphins can swim around and sleep at the same time.

Five tips that might help you get a good night's sleep
1. Try to go to bed and wake up at the same times to get your body used to a routine.
2. Avoid soda, because it often contains caffeine, which may keep you awake.
3. If you can, try to do a little exercise every day, but not just before bedtime.
4. Have a bath before you go to bed—the heat will help your body relax.
5. If you cannot sleep, do not lie awake thinking about it. Try reading a book in bed.

Your age affects how much sleep you need. Babies need about 16 hours of sleep, adults about eight hours, and elderly people often need as little as four hours. You probably need about 10 hours of sleep—the same as a dog!

Dreaming

People have always been fascinated by the strange and shadowy world of dreams and have tried to make sense of them in all kinds of different ways.

The Native American Ojibwas, or Chippewas, hang magical webs, called dream catchers, from babies' cradles. They are made from willow hoops, plant fibers, and feathers, which symbolize breath or air. It is believed that the webs catch all the bad dreams, but allow good dreams to slip through to the babies.

In the ancient world dreams were believed to be messages from the gods—warnings or predictions that were taken very seriously. Special dream interpreters (often priests or priestesses) were used to decode these divine communications and to unravel all their mysteries.

Today scientists believe sleep is divided into dreaming and nondreaming. Each night, when you drift off to sleep, your brain runs on autopilot, chewing things over. After about 90 minutes you emerge from deep sleep and enter dreaming sleep. This is when you have those hair-raising adventures, strange encounters, and odd experiences like running furiously and getting nowhere, flying high in the sky, or falling into a dark, bottomless pit.

Scientists in special sleep laboratories conduct research on patterns of sleep and dreaming. They glue small electrodes to the scalps of volunteers to detect brain activity and to areas around the eyes to monitor eye movement. The information is recorded and analyzed.

14

Today some people still believe that dreams have important meanings. By analyzing the content of your dreams, they think that they can reveal something about an aspect of your life or even predict something about your future.

If you dream of pirates, you will have an adventure.

A dream about ice cream means you will be successful.

Dream of an ear and you will hear startling news.

Dreaming of strawberries brings happiness.

An umbrella is a symbol of security.

Dreaming of birds is lucky.

During dream sleep the body is paralyzed by the brain and will not move at all except for rapid eye movements and twitches of hands or feet. This paralysis protects the body from injury by allowing the sleeper to dream about adventurous activities without actually performing them in bed!

Dreaming sleep is also known as Rapid Eye Movement (REM) sleep because your eyes move around beneath your eyelids while you are dreaming. REM lasts for about 20 minutes and occurs at least five times every night, causing vivid dreams—even if you don't remember them!

Pajama party

If you are very lucky (and very nice to your parents) every once in a while you may be allowed to stay up past your bedtime for a pajama party or a midnight feast!

Sneak down to the kitchen for some nighttime nibbles. A midnight menu should be simple—avoid rich foods, such as cheese and chocolate, which are hard to digest late at night.

Pajamas, which come from India, were originally worn around the house during the day. The word "pajamas" comes from the ancient Persian and Urdu for leg (*pae*) and clothing (*jamah*).

Plan your sleepover party carefully. It is best to have it at the weekend or during school vacations, so that you do not have to wake up very early the next day. Don't invite too many people—it is more fun with just your closest friends.

No pajama party is complete without games. To play Telephone, everyone sits in a circle, and one person thinks up a sentence—it could be funny, tongue-twisting, or spooky. The sentence is whispered from person to person around the circle. The last person to hear the message has to say it out loud. How much has the message changed from its original version?

To play Wink Murder, get a few slips of paper—the same number as there are players. Write "M" for murderer on one, "D" for detective on another, and leave the rest blank. Fold up the pieces of paper, and let everyone choose one, reading the slips in secret. Then everyone sits in a circle and silently looks at one another. The murderer can murder people by winking at them. If you are winked at, fake a dramatic death, and remain dead for the rest of the game. The murderer must try to murder everyone without being caught by the detective, who must catch the murderer winking and reveal their identity to win the game.

Ghost stories can be loads of fun. Turn off the lights and tell some spooky tales. But remember they are only stories—nothing to be afraid of!

Shine a flashlight or bedside light against a wall and try to make these hand shadows. Can you invent any others?

Standing between the light and the wall, bend your arm into the shape of a swan's neck. Make the head and beak with your hand.

Cross your hands over each other and link your thumbs. Can you see a bird, butterfly, or nighttime bat? Try to make it flap its wings.

Make a dog shadow by bending your index finger and sticking your thumb up. Then lower your little finger to open the dog's mouth.

An A to Z of night fun

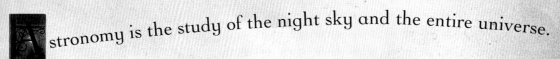

We associate all kinds of things with night — stars, ghosts, and UFOs. When you separate the facts from the fiction, the night can be a lot of fun!

Astronomy is the study of the night sky and the entire universe.

Baba Yaga, a witch of Russian folklore, flies through the air in a kettle!

Candles made from beeswax or animal fat lit homes at night long ago.

Darkness is nothing to fear — it just makes things a little harder to see!

Equinox, "equal night," occurs when night and day are the same length.

Frogs often croak loud nighttime choruses to try to attract mates.

Ghosts are spooky spirits that some people think come out at night.

Hecate is the ancient Greek goddess of ghosts, magic, and witches.

Imps are tiny fantasy figures that may play naughty nighttime tricks!

Jack-o'-lanterns are made out of hollowed-out pumpkins at Halloween.

Kakapos are night parrots from New Zealand that look like owls.

Lantern festivals light the darkness in many parts the world.

Moonrats are tiny, hairy, Asian mammals that creep out at night.

Nightmares were once thought to be monsters sitting on people's chests.

Owl monkeys, or night monkeys, have large, round, yellow eyes.

Poltergeists are spirits that some people blame for nighttime noises.

Quivering and quaking? But there is no need to be afraid of the night!

Radishes are sculpted and celebrated on a special night in Mexico!

Stars twinkle and sparkle in the vast darkness of our night skies.

Twilight is the soft light that falls between sunset and darkness.

UFOs, unidentified flying objects, are sometimes seen at night.

Vampires are fantasy creatures that drink blood and hate daylight.

Werewolves are fictional people who turn into wolves during a full moon.

X,Y,Z are x-files, yetis, and . . . zzz, zzz . . . time for bed!

Night Lights

Long ago, before electricity and lightbulbs
arrived, nights could be as black as ink.
Lighting the darkness has always been
a matter of necessity, but also of pleasure —
think about the importance of a lighthouse,
guiding ships into port, or the beauty of
a firework display, illuminating the skies
in every direction for miles around.

The lighthouse

For thousands of years light has been used as a signal. From the top of lighthouses fires burned brightly to guide ships at sea, and bonfires blazed from hilltops to warn of invasion. Today lighthouses send out very powerful beams of electric light.

Lighthouses flash their powerful lights over the night seas to guide ships toward harbor or away from rocks. Most boats and ships have on-board navigation systems, but sailors still rely on the comforting glow from a lighthouse if their systems fail! The beam from a lighthouse is reflected through lenses and shone directly at the horizon—no light is wasted by being sent toward the sky or the sea. The strength of the beam is measured in "candelas"—a beam of 100,000 candelas can be seen about 25 miles (10km) away.

The first known lighthouse was built more than 2,000 years ago on the island of Pharos in the ancient port of Alexandria, Egypt. At more than 325 feet (100m) high, it was the Earth's tallest structure. From its top a huge fire blazed, turning the night sky a deep red. It is thought that a metal mirror reflected the light from the fire up to 30 miles (50km). The lighthouse had three main sections—a box-shaped column, and a central octagonal pillar with a cylinder on top. Clad in dazzling white marble, this amazing structure is one of the Seven Wonders of the Ancient World.

Lighthouses are beacons—light signals used to communicate messages. In the past beacons were usually small fires. Chains of beacons were used as early-warning systems. The beacons were lit one by one on hilltops, towers, and walls to pass news over long distances—sometimes hundreds of miles. In 1588 the Spanish Armada —a fleet of 130 ships—was spotted approaching England, and a chain of bonfires was lit along the English coast to warn of the attack.

Perhaps the most famous beacon is the Olympic flame. Every four years a torch is lit from the sun's rays in the ancient stadium in Olympia, Greece, where the Olympic Games began more than three thousand years ago. Over several months thousands of runners relay the torch through many countries to the opening ceremony of the Games. For the 2000 Olympics in Sydney, Australia, the flame briefly traveled underwater, carried as a burning flare by a scuba diver.

Night shine

To get by in our nighttime world, we rely on many different forms of light—from tiny reflectors that wink light along dark roads to huge neon signs that shine their messages to whole cities.

Luminous things glow in the dark. Some reflect light given off by other objects —road signs shine when they reflect the light from car headlights. Shiny, smooth, bright materials, such as mirrors, make the best reflectors.

Lightbulbs produce their own light when electric currents are passed through wires inside the bulbs. Electricity can also cause gases such as neon to glow orange and red.

Ultraviolet light is a form of radiation, which makes some materials glow in the dark. Some people label their belongings with special ink, visible only under ultraviolet light, so they can be identified if stolen and then recovered.

The electric lights of Las Vegas dominate the skyline of the Nevada desert. The city buzzes and glows with activity nonstop— you can shop, visit a casino, and even get married in the middle of the night! Along a road known as "The Strip," 15,500 miles (25,000km) of neon tubes and thousands of lightbulbs create amazing displays—there is a huge exploding volcano and a replica of France's Eiffel Tower!

Luminous watches glow in the dark so that we can tell the time during the night. The hands and numbers on their faces are coated with a special chemical that produces light. Televisions and computer monitors also glow in the dark. Their screens are made up of tiny dots that glow red, green, or blue. From a distance, moving, color pictures are seen.

Reflectors lie at intervals along the middle of the road and reflect the headlights of cars at night so drivers can follow the bends in the road ahead. The reflectors are reinforced glass, shaped to reflect as much light as brightly as possible. The glass is protected in rubber cups and sunk into the road.

Fireworks

From a tiny sparkler twinkling in the night to a huge rocket exploding into a thousand shining stars, fireworks are used all over the world in celebrations. They have beautiful, exotic, or even scary names— Silver Rain, Jeweled Pyramid, or Mine of Serpents.

Fireworks were probably invented in ancient China, where gunpowder was discovered 2,000 years ago. One ingredient of gunpowder is saltpeter, which is found throughout China and other parts of Asia. Saltpeter, or Chinese snow, is still used to make fireworks. It is mixed with charcoal and sulfur and packed into hollow paper tubes to create the most traditional of all fireworks—rockets.

A rocket is launched when the fuse attached to the gunpowder mixture inside is lit. The jet of fire and gases produced propels the rocket into the sky. Once the rocket is in the air, further explosions cause a spectacular firework display.

Fireworks probably spread to Europe in the 1200s, but it wasn't until the 1800s, when new chemicals were added to the original gunpowder recipe, that a variety of sparkles and stars, bangs and hisses became possible. It was discovered that different chemical compounds produce different colors — compounds of sodium produce yellow, strontium red, barium green, and compounds of copper, mixed with chlorine gas, produce blue.

Firecrackers that produced loud bangs and only tiny sparks were the earliest form of modern fireworks. They were first used in ancient China to honor the gods and to celebrate weddings, births, battle victories, and eclipses of the moon. Their most important use was to frighten evil spirits away from homes—a tradition still practiced in China today.

Firework displays are also called pyrotechnics, which means "skill with fire" in ancient Greek.

Early fireworks were adapted from military rockets and missiles, and some forms of fireworks are still used today in warfare—star shells are used to light up battlefields, and parachute flares illuminate landing areas for aircraft. Other flares and rockets are used as warning or distress signals, and many sailors or mountaineers carry them in case of emergency.

WARNING: All fireworks are dangerous. They can and do cause serious injury. They must be set off by adults only. In many places, fireworks are illegal and can only be handled by experts during organized pyrotechnic displays.

SPECIAL NIGHTS

Throughout the ages people from all over the world have had different ideas about the night. While some have feared it, most have enjoyed its magic and mystery. Festivals, both religious and nonreligious, often take place at night, making use of the darkness to celebrate light—a symbol of goodness and truth in many cultures.

January to February

The new year is welcomed with spectacular festivals all over the world. Chinese New Year arrives with a bang in either January or February, depending on a calendar based on the cycles of the moon. A little later the Rio Carnival kicks off in fantastic style.

The leader of the dragon dance entices the dragon with a giant "pearl" (a balloon or lantern).

Chinese New Year is the most important festival for Chinese families all over the world. It is a time of peace, happiness, and success. Houses are cleaned to sweep away bad luck from the previous year and to welcome in good luck for the next.

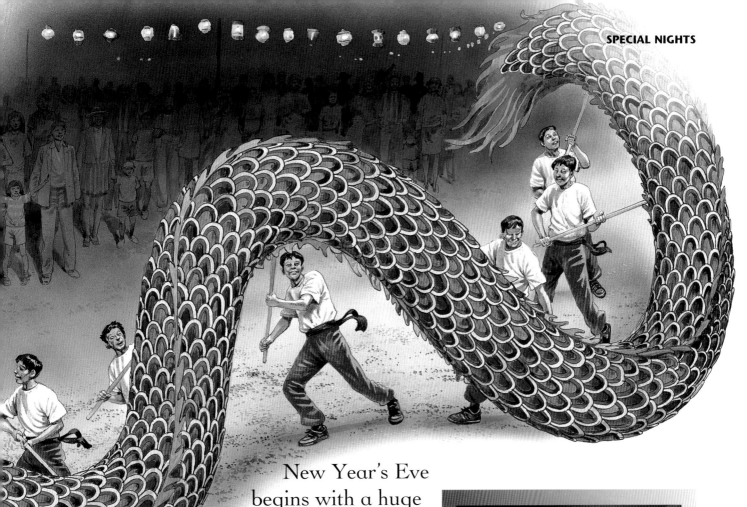

New Year's Eve begins with a huge feast for all the family —there are even places set at the table for the spirits of departed ancestors. The menu might include sharks' fins, birds' nests, sea cucumbers, and jellyfish. Red lanterns glow all night, and firecrackers are set off at midnight. This is said to scare off Nian, a legendary monster who is terrified of light, the color red, and loud noises.

Fifteen days later the celebrations close with the Lantern Festival, during which beautiful lanterns light the streets. Often there is a dragon dance—a huge dragon made of silk, paper, and bamboo weaves through the crowds, led by skilled dancers.

The spectacular Rio Carnival is held every year in Rio de Janeiro, Brazil. A huge parade of floats and samba dancers, wearing fantastic feathery costumes, weaves its way down the grandest avenue in Rio. The carnival is a Christian Mardi Gras festival, a chance to feast and party before Lent, when some Christians avoid rich food or meat for 40 days. The word carnival comes from the Latin phrase *carne vale*, which means "good-bye meat."

31

March to April

The beginning of spring is celebrated by two very different festivals of fire. In India, Hindus gather around bonfires to celebrate Holi. At around the same time, the Spanish city of Valencia is lit up for five days during Las Fallas, or "The Fires."

Holi begins on the night of the full moon during the spring harvest. Worshipers gather wood and pile it into huge mounds. Then priests say prayers before lighting the fires. The flames are thought to point toward land that will be fertile the next year. As the bonfires blaze away, some people sing, beat drums, or play horns.

The Holi bonfire is connected to an ancient story about a demon named Holika and her nephew, the noble prince Prahlad. They both walked into a bonfire, but only Prahlad escaped unharmed.

Offerings of wheat, grain, popcorn, incense, and garlands of flowers are placed around the bonfire and later thrown into it. Coconuts (symbols of new life) are roasted in the fire and then eaten as prasada, or "holy food."

Holi is also a festival of color—a symbol of fertility. People cover each other in brightly colored powdered paints known as gulal. They mix the powders with water and squirt them from water pistols and bicycle pumps. Jokes and pranks are played, and everyone has a chance to have fun in the colorful mess.

Cows are sacred in India, so their dung is holy too. Garlands of cow dung are thrown into some Holi bonfires.

At the beginning of Las Fallas, elaborate statues of historical figures, animals, and even pop stars are made from wood and plaster and displayed all over Valencia. Many are as tall as buildings and need to be put into place by cranes. On March 19, the feast day of Saint Joseph, crowds gather for the final night of celebrations. The statues are stuffed with fireworks, and the streetlights are turned off. At the stroke of midnight, all the statues—often more than 300 in total—are set on fire. Only the crowd's favorite is spared from the flames.

May to June

Tikkun leyl Shavuot is a special night of quiet study for devout Jews, and the candlelit Visakha festival is an important and solemn occasion for Buddhists in Thailand. However, Midsummer's Night in Scandinavia is a lively and loud event with singing and dancing under the midnight sun.

Tikkun leyl Shavuot is a religious book as well as the name for the night the book is read. At night heaven is said to receive prayers, so Jews try to pray and read all night. They may have milk and honey, symbols of the Torah—the teachings God delivered to Moses.

Visakha honors the day of the year on which it is thought that Buddha was born, enlightened (released from the sufferings of the mind), and died. At dusk worshipers bring candles, incense, and food to monasteries, which they walk around three times as part of the ceremony.

Midsummer's Night in the Northern Hemisphere falls around June 21, when this part of earth is tilted directly toward the sun and receives more sunlight than on any other day. This is the summer solstice—the longest day of the whole year—when night becomes day.

Sweden, Norway, Denmark, and Finland are all part of Scandinavia, which sits high in the Northern Hemisphere. They have celebrated Midsummer's Night for thousands of years. The night marks the return of summer and a new season of crops. Many people head to beautiful areas among the mountains and lakes. They watch the sun, which at midnight just touches the horizon but does not set.

Midsummer's Night is a time of festive fun. Men, women, and children dance around maypoles, wearing traditional costumes and garlands made from flowers and leaves— symbols of new life. Everyone celebrates by dancing, singing, and feasting on homemade beer and cheese.

Maypoles are often shaped like Christian crosses because the birth of St. John the Baptist is also celebrated on Midsummer's Night.

Accordion players provide music for the maypole dance. Some maypoles have colorful ribbons that are woven around the pole by the dancers.

July to August

In the warm nights of July and August two very special events take place. The Star Festival in Japan remembers two star-crossed lovers, and Sri Lanka's Esala Perahera, with its magnificent procession of elephants, is unmissable.

Every year, on one night in the Buddhist month of Esala (July or August), the streets of Kandy in Sri Lanka are filled with dancers, drummers, acrobats, fire-eaters, and, most importantly, elephants. They all gather to celebrate the final procession of the spectacular Esala Perahera— a two-week festival held in honor of a single tooth. It is believed that this tooth belonged to Buddha himself.

When Buddha, the Enlightened One, died about 2,500 years ago, it is thought that one of his teeth was taken from his funeral pyre and brought to Sri Lanka, hidden in the hair of a princess. Today the tooth, known as the Relic, is kept in a golden casket in the Dalada Maligawa—the Temple of the Tooth.

The lead elephant walks on a carpet of white linen so that it remains pure, its feet never touching the earth.

On the final night of the festival, when the moon is full, a replica of the Relic is paraded through the streets. It sits proudly under a canopy of electric lights, carried on an elephant known as the Maligawa Tusker. This distinguished elephant is the leader of almost 100 elephants, all decorated in beautiful cloths and bright lights. The city echoes with the sound of drums, cracking whips, the clanging of the elephants' bells, and the cheers of the delighted spectators.

The Japanese Star Festival, Tanabata, takes place on July 7. The celebration relates to an ancient Chinese myth about two lovers—Vega and Altair. They were banished to the heavens to become stars separated by the Milky Way. Vega and Altair can reunite only once a year—on July 7. On this day, young lovers, some in beautiful traditional dress, meet under the stars. The city of Sendai celebrates Tanabata over three days in August. Love poems and wishes are written on paper streamers and attached to bamboo sticks. These colorful decorations frame lively street parades.

Talented drummers and dancers perform at the festival. Originally the Kandyan classical dancing skills were handed down within families from father to son. Today anyone with talent and dedication can train to become a dancer.

37

September to October

The magical Chinese Moon Festival and Divali, the Hindu festival of lights, both cheer the gloom at this time of year. But Halloween, celebrated all over the world, delights in the darkness and is certainly the spookiest night of the year.

It is traditional to eat tasty mooncakes made from pastry and delicious fillings during the Chinese Moon Festival, also known as the Harvest Festival. Families picnic at night, eating the cakes, drinking tea, and honoring the moon—a symbol of abundance and harmony.

Divali (or Deepavali) means "row of lights," and during this festival divas, which are tiny clay lamps, are lit after sunset. The lamps welcome home king Rama, who was in exile for 14 years and conquered the demon Ravana. Divali, which celebrates all triumphs of good over evil, is also associated with Lakshmi, the goddess of wealth.

The tradition of Halloween stretches back for many centuries to the ancient Celtic festival of Samhain, which means summer's end. Samhain took place on October 31, the last night of the Celtic year. It was a time of witches and warlocks and the ghosts of departed souls who were thought to revisit the earth, seeking revenge.

Halloween takes its name from the Christian adaptation of Samhain—All Hallow's Eve ("hallowed" means holy). However, this night has always been associated more with death, evil, and the supernatural than with Christian beliefs. Over time harmless creatures, such as bats, black cats, and spiders have developed spooky reputations and are now symbols of Halloween. Mythical beings such as werewolves and vampires are also feared on this night. Although people still enjoy old superstitions, today Halloween is a festival of fun, not fear.

Trick-or-treating
is a popular Halloween
tradition. Children in
costumes visit local homes,
asking for candy and other treats
under the playful threat of tricks.
After trick-or-treating, children
sometimes go to Halloween parties
and play games, such as bobbing
for apples. There may even be
a pretend fortune teller and a
scary haunted house. Children
should always be accompanied
by adults when trick-or-treating.

The carved,
candlelit pumpkin—
the jack-o'-lantern—probably
relates to a character named Jack
in Irish folklore. When Jack, who was
very mischievous, died he wasn't
allowed into heaven. He wasn't
allowed into hell, either, because he had
even tricked the devil! Instead, Jack was
doomed to walk the earth with only
a glowing ember in a hollowed-out
turnip to light his way through
the darkness.

November to December

On December 31, at the stroke of midnight, people all over the world celebrate the start of a new year. In London, England, crowds gather near Big Ben, a historic clock tower, to watch the clock strike midnight.

As the year comes to an end the nighttime festivities continue. Important Muslim and Jewish festivals take place, Mexico honors its dead, and England remembers Guy Fawkes with blazing bonfires.

Eid-ul-Fitr is the huge celebration that marks the end of Ramadan, the ninth and most holy month of the Muslim year. The exact date for this festival varies because the Muslim calendar is lunar—based on the cycles of the moon. Ramadan is very holy because during this month about 1,400 years ago, the prophet Muhammad received the first revelation from Allah (God). During Ramadan, Muslims fast from dawn to sunset—they only eat or drink at night. Eid-ul-Fitr, which means the "Festival of the Breaking of the Fast," begins when the new moon of the next month, Shawwal, is sighted.

The crescent of the new moon is a faint sliver and is often very difficult to see. People search the night skies with binoculars or small telescopes from high spots around the cities and towns. As soon as they have seen the moon, they contact religious leaders, called muftis, who organize the official announcement of the end of Ramadan on TV and radio stations.

That night Muslims all over the world prepare for the festivities of the following day, when families will enjoy a daytime meal for the first time in a month. They clean their houses and put on their best clothes, then they are ready to receive visitors. They also make gifts and cards to exchange as symbols of blessings and joy. The next morning, just after the sun has risen, special prayers in the mosques begin the day.

In Mexico, November 1 and 2 are Days of the Dead. People spend entire nights beside their relatives' graves. They decorate the graves with sugar skeletons and with candles to guide souls back to Earth.

November 5 is Bonfire Night in England. Bonfires are lit to remember Guy Fawkes who tried—and failed—to blow up the English Parliament on this day in 1605. Straw dummies, or guys, sit on top of the bonfires.

Hanukkah, the Festival of Lights celebrating the Jewish faith, falls in December. Every night for eight nights, families light a candle on the eight-branched menorah using a central candle, called a shamash.

41

NIGHT NATURE

When night falls another world comes
to life in the jungles, deserts, dark skies,
and deep oceans. We know about many
of the plants and animals that thrive
in these nighttime kingdoms, but some
remain a mystery. You may never see
a shadowy night creature, because most
are shyer than you, but a rustle, hoot,
or howl will tell you it's nearby.

Nighttime plants

For a few plants our night is their day. Their sweet-smelling flowers open as the sun goes down, and they are visited by night-flying insects in search of nectar.

Most flowers open their petals during the day so that they can be pollinated by bees and other daytime insects. When it gets dark, these flowers close their petals to protect their pollen from rain and dew. Insects may get trapped inside the petals, but it's a warm, safe place to spend the night.

The Queen of the Night, or Moon cactus is a very unusual plant. It flowers for only one night every year. Some people stay up all night to watch its huge, white petals, which can be 8 inches (20cm) long, unfold. By morning the fragrant blooms will have died—until the next year.

The flowers of night-blooming plants are usually ghostly white or the palest yellow or pink— colors that contrast well with the gathering gloom. These colors help moths find the blooms, but as it gets darker it is the flowers' scents that guide the moths in the right direction. Many flowers, such as butterfly orchids and honeysuckles, have faint smells during the day, but their nighttime perfumes are very strong.

The long, spindly flowers of the honeysuckle make it difficult for most insects to drink the sugary nectar that is inside of them. But they are perfectly designed for night-feeding hawk moths, which have long, thin tongues called proboscises, which they can insert into the tubes of the flowers.

Flowers that have sour, musty smells attract bats. Hovering like hummingbirds next to the flowers, the bats use their long, wriggly tongues to drink the nectar. Many flowers rely on bats and moths for pollination. The powdery pollen clings onto the nighttime visitors and later rubs off on either the same flower or different flowers, fertilizing them and causing the plants to reproduce.

Nighttime animals

As you turn off the lights and go to sleep another world outside your window wakes up and goes to work. Owls hoot, mice scuttle, bats swoop, and slugs slide.

Animals that are awake at night are nocturnal. They search for food, find mates, and avoid being eaten by predators in almost complete darkness. Fortunately they have adapted to life with little light, and they each have at least one sense—sight, smell, hearing, taste, or touch—that is exceptionally good.

Small nocturnal mammals such as hedgehogs have a very good sense of smell. Some animals have large eyes to make the most of every available speck of light.

Some creatures find it easier to hunt at night, when there is less competition around. Bats and nightjars scoop up flying insects that feed swifts and swallows during the day. Owls swoop on mice and small birds, which kestrels try to snatch in daylight hours. It is just like working in shifts!

Creepy crawlies, such as wood lice, centipedes, snails, and slugs, prefer the dark because it is cool and damp. Their skins are not waterproof, and they would lose too much moisture if they came out of their hiding places during the day.

Nightjars are very graceful birds. As they fly they open their beaks, or bills, to try to catch insects.

The red fox is very intelligent. It can adapt to living in woodland, open countryside, and even cities.

At dusk badgers emerge from their setts, or burrows. They eat mostly fruit, nuts, and earthworms.

Snails and slugs leave behind trails of slime as they make their way around damp nighttime gardens.

Raccoons are usually found in towns and cities at night. They search through trash cans looking for food.

Hedgehogs have thick, prickly coats. When a hedgehog senses danger, it curls up into a tight, prickly ball.

Seeing in the dark

Creatures that come out in the dark of the night usually have much better night vision than humans do. On a black, moonless night owls, leopards, bush babies, and pet cats can see shadowy shapes that help them find their way around, hunt for food, and hide from danger.

Some animals, such as the African bush baby, have a layer of cells called a tapetum at the back of their eyes. The tapetum acts like a mirror, reflecting light. This causes eyeshine—when eyes glow like shiny sequins.

The African leopard, like all members of the cat family, has very good night vision. This powerful hunter preys on baboons and antelope and any small animals that it can find in the darkness of the bush.

The eyes of nocturnal animals are designed to make the most of whatever light is available. Their eyes are usually very big, with large lenses and extremely sensitive retinas. The retina is the lining at the back of the eye that sends messages to the brain, which then interprets what has been seen.

As far as we know, nocturnal animals can see only in black and white and shades of gray. This is because the light-sensitive cells of their retinas are shaped like rods rather than cones. Rod-shaped cells can detect only whether there is any light or not; the cone-shaped cells detect color. The retinas of humans contain both rods and cones.

The eyes of some night hunters are so big that they can't move around in their sockets at all. This means that the creature has to turn its whole head to follow moving objects. Owls, with their huge, saucerlike eyes, can swivel their heads all the way around to stare directly behind them.

The pupil is the hole in the center of the iris—the colored part of the eye. During the day the cat's narrow pupils stop too much bright daylight from entering the eye and damaging the retina.

During the night a cat's pupils widen and become rounded. This enables as much of the dim light as possible to pass through the pupils to the retinas, helping the cat see better in the dark.

49

Night Owl

Most owls are efficient and skillful hunters perfectly designed to swoop silently through the dark night skies. This barn owl, with its distinctive heart-shaped face, is no exception. The owl's body is small and light, but its wings are huge and powerful and are covered with a velvety down that muffles sound and gives no warning to its victims.

Large, round eyes on flat faces give owls excellent binocular vision in the dimmest light, but it is their finely tuned sense of hearing that can pick up the tiniest rustle of a dry leaf or the faintest snap of a twig from great distances through the still night air.

The barn owl is sometimes called the monkey-faced owl because of its beady eyes and comical behavior. Found all over the world, it is a familiar nocturnal owl and is often known simply as the night owl.

When the barn owl detects its prey, it plunges, powerful talons outstretched, and snatches its favorite food— a mouse, rat, frog, or bird.

There are about 130 different species of owls found all over the world. The burrowing owl, from North and South America, lives in abandoned burrows, which it guards during the day. If it is disturbed, it makes buzzing calls to mimic a rattlesnake. During the night the burrowing owl hunts; because it does not like to fly, it runs along the ground on long, specially adapted legs.

The Australian sooty owl is rarely seen or heard in its dense rain forest habitat. This most striking owl is soot-colored with huge dark eyes, but perhaps is best known for its unusual bomb-whistle call, which sounds like a bomb falling without the final explosion.

The female long-eared owl, from Europe, North America, and Africa, is a fierce defender of her nest. She will distract intruders by pretending to be injured or by flopping around on the ground away from her nest, making strange noises. If this fails, she will spread her wings into a huge fan to appear twice as big — terrifying any raccoon or hostile owl that crosses her path!

With sharp, hooked beaks, owls tear their prey to pieces and swallow it in chunks. They spit out compact pellets of fur, feathers, bone, and anything else they can't digest.

Night bat

At sunset huge colonies of bats emerge from caves, spiraling in dark clouds high into the sky. The flapping of thousands of pairs of wings sends cool breezes through the night air. A spectacular sight visible for miles, the bats are off to hunt insects and will return just before sunrise.

There are nearly 1,000 species of bats—from Thailand's tiny bumblebee bat to Indonesia's giant flying fox, which has a wingspan of almost six feet (2m). Some bats swoop over lakes and rivers to catch fish, while others drink the nectar from desert cacti. Their scientific Latin name is *chiroptera*, meaning "hand-wings," and bats are the only mammals that can truly fly.

Fruit bats, or flying foxes, are large bats with foxlike faces. They live in small groups in trees and feast on soft fruits.

The world's largest bat colony—
20 to 40 million Mexican free-tailed
bats—lives in Bracken Cave in Texas.
Every night, they produce tons of
droppings, or guano, which can be
used to make fertilizers, insecticides,
and medicines. No wonder witch
doctors once believed bats were
magical and could cure disease!

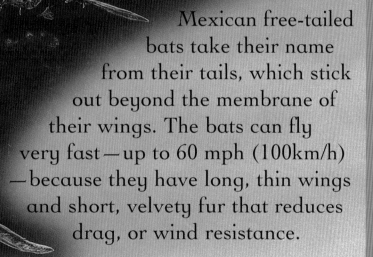

Bats hang upside
down from the roofs
of caves, safely above
danger. They drop into
the space below them
to swoop into flight.

Vampire bats use
their razor-sharp
teeth to bite cattle.
Their saliva makes
blood flow freely so
they can lap it up.

Old-man bats have
very wrinkly faces!
The wrinkles help the
bats make squeaking
noises with their
mouths and noses.

Mexican free-tailed
bats take their name
from their tails, which stick
out beyond the membrane of
their wings. The bats can fly
very fast—up to 60 mph (100km/h)
—because they have long, thin wings
and short, velvety fur that reduces
drag, or wind resistance.

The bats hunt moths with the help of echolocation,
which enables them to "see" in the dark. Every
second the bats emit between 10 and 20 squeaks—
too high-pitched for humans to hear—and then
listen for the returning echoes with their large
ears. Different objects send back different
echoes, and the bats can use this information
to build up a picture of their surroundings.

Creepy Crawlies

You probably share your home with a few tiny creatures that emerge when you are fast asleep. These harmless houseguests may leave behind some clues— a trail of droppings, miniature footprints, or a silk web.

All moths are attracted to lights. The beautiful Moon moth's four wings are covered in tiny green scales that give the moth its striking color. The scales rub off easily, and as the moth gets older it will become duller in color.

Wood lice, which are also called sow bugs or pill bugs, emerge from their damp hiding places at night to feed on rotten wood or decaying plants. They are nicknamed "roly-polies" because they can roll up into tight balls, protecting themselves inside armor-plated globes.

Crickets are also attracted to lights and often gather around them, disturbing anyone trying to sleep with their loud chirping chorus. Only male crickets make this noise, rubbing their wings together in order to attract females.

Cockroaches are happiest in warm surroundings, although they can survive freezing temperatures. Some cockroaches have fully developed wings that they use to glide around in the air. Cockroaches are troublesome creatures that can spread germs. They eat anything they can find—from shoe polish, soap, and ink to glue and wallpaper!

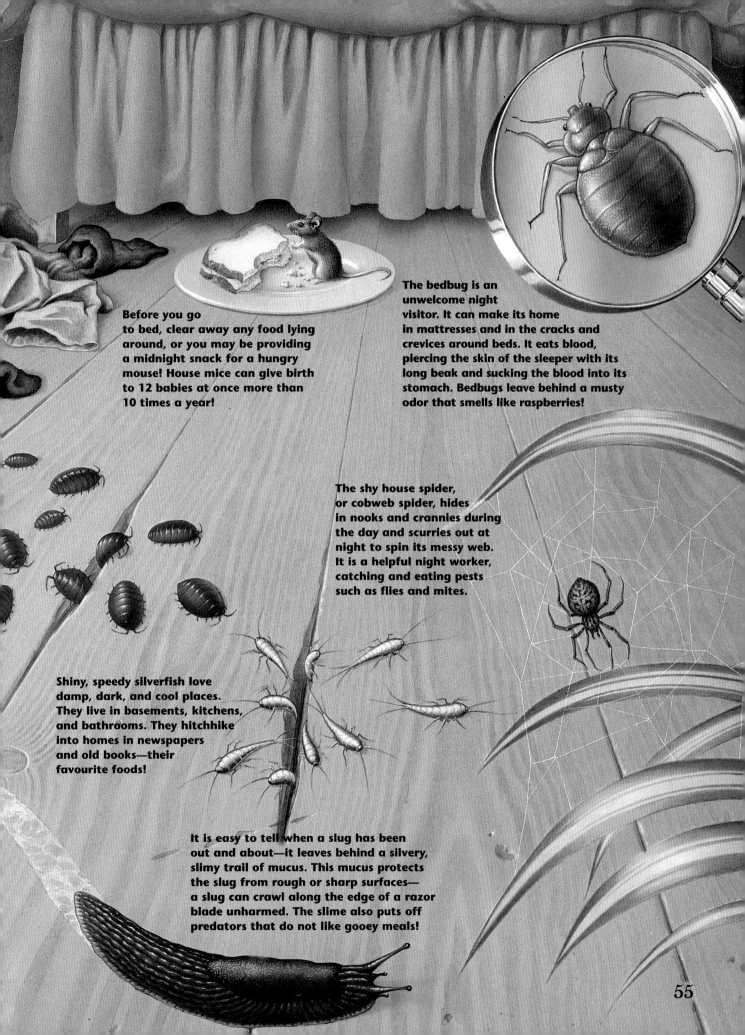

Before you go
to bed, clear away any food lying
around, or you may be providing
a midnight snack for a hungry
mouse! House mice can give birth
to 12 babies at once more than
10 times a year!

The bedbug is an
unwelcome night
visitor. It can make its home
in mattresses and in the cracks and
crevices around beds. It eats blood,
piercing the skin of the sleeper with its
long beak and sucking the blood into its
stomach. Bedbugs leave behind a musty
odor that smells like raspberries!

The shy house spider,
or cobweb spider, hides
in nooks and crannies during
the day and scurries out at
night to spin its messy web.
It is a helpful night worker,
catching and eating pests
such as flies and mites.

Shiny, speedy silverfish love
damp, dark, and cool places.
They live in basements, kitchens,
and bathrooms. They hitchhike
into homes in newspapers
and old books—their
favourite foods!

It is easy to tell when a slug has been
out and about—it leaves behind a silvery,
slimy trail of mucus. This mucus protects
the slug from rough or sharp surfaces—
a slug can crawl along the edge of a razor
blade unharmed. The slime also puts off
predators that do not like gooey meals!

A night in the desert

When the scorching desert sun sets, an army of creatures emerges to look for food. By day they hide from the heat under rocks or in burrows, but in the cool night air they venture out onto the bleak, moonlit landscape.

The desert at night can be a hostile place, and many animals survive with special skills or weapons. The gila monster is a fearsome lizard with striking yellow and black markings that warn its enemies and prey of its poisonous bite. A rattlesnake, shaking the rattle at the tip of its tail, can also deliver a venomous bite. Scorpions don't bite, but they do have a poisonous stinger at the end of their abdomen.

The coyote, with its mournful howl, is a skilled hunter. As a member of the canine family, it has an excellent sense of smell and hearing and can run very fast.

The desert porcupine has quills that it can thrust into an attacker. The quills remain stuck in the victim, and it can take several months for new quills to grow back.

The tiny African fennec fox has huge ears that act like radiators, giving off excess heat to keep the fox cool. The fennec lives in an underground burrow during the day.

The hairy sun spider is a fierce hunter, devouring lizards, mice, and small birds. The spider, which makes its nest with animal hair, bites off the legs of its prey before eating it.

The bobcat, like the coyote, preys
on small mammals such as jackrabbits
and kangaroo rats. A kangaroo rat
will put up a bold defense against such
predators, kicking sand in their faces
and hopping around in all directions,
using its long tail to balance.
The tiny elf owl prefers to
fly away from its enemies
to hidden perches in
cacti rather than
stay and fight.

A night at Sea

When the sun's rays have dimmed and the oceans turn an inky black, different sea creatures glow and shine in the darkness. Sea fire sparkles on the surface of tropical waters, and in the depths squid glow while flashlight fish rotate their lights to search for food, safe from daytime predators.

Sea fire, or phosphorescence, carpets the sea in a glittering, orange light. It is produced by thousands of tiny sea organisms called plankton. The plankton glow when they are moved around by the waves; and perhaps by schools of dolphins using echolocation to search for fish in the dark.

For the creatures that inhabit the deepest ocean depths there is no difference between night and day—they live in permanent darkness. Many deep-sea fish are blind and feel their way around with tiny sensors. Others have special taste buds that tell them about their surroundings. Some fish have eyes that face up so they can peer at the dim silhouettes and shadows near the surface.

The transparent bell and short tentacles of the moon jellyfish seem to glow a milky white in the dark. The jellyfish expands and contracts its bell to push water out and propel itself along.

The wobbegong shark, or carpet shark, hunts for fish in the night. During the day it lies on the ocean floor and uses the fringes around its mouth to disguise itself as seaweed.

The seahorse is a very unusual marine animal—the male seahorse gives birth! He will anchor himself to coral with his curly tail so that the female seahorse can lay her eggs in his pouch.

The bat starfish, like many starfish, can tell night from day by using the light-sensitive tips on the end of each arm. Some starfish are drawn to the light, while others prefer to stay in the dark.

Some anglerfish disguise themselves as seaweed and lure fish into their mouths with fins that look like worms. Deep-sea anglerfish have lights on the end of these "fishing rods" to attract fish.

Cuttlefish put on one of the best underwater light shows. If they are agitated, electric blue spots and flashes of light pulse along their bodies. The colors are made by small sacks in their skin.

Nature glows

The nighttime darkness of dense, tropical rain forests is lit by bioluminescence—light that is produced naturally by all kinds of different plants and insects.

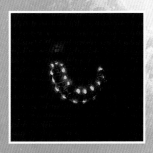

Fireflies are nocturnal winged beetles that use light signals to attract mates. The orange or green glows from their abdomens are produced by chemical reactions.

The rare railroad worm from South America is a firefly larva. It has a red glowing "headlamp" and rows of luminous green spots along its body that look like railroad signals.

The cucujo beetle is the most luminous insect of all. Long ago they were used instead of candles, and people tied them to their feet to light their way. Girls even wore them as hair decorations!

Fireflies, found all over the world, are a common cause of natural, nighttime glows. Their luminous, wormlike offspring, or larvae, are known as glowworms, as are some female wingless fireflies. They gather in trees in the thousands, continuously flashing their lights in time with each other, sometimes for months on end.

The yellow jack-o'-lantern mushroom produces a greenish glow from the gills on its underside. Like many fungi, it is poisonous.

Mushrooms known as fox fire glow blue, yellow, and green on damp forest floors. The petals of the moon flower are so white that they seem to glow in the moonlight.

One centipede from Asia produces luminous secretions between its segments, giving it a striped glow. Mammals and amphibians are not bioluminescent—but some frogs eat so many fireflies that they glow from the inside!

NIGHT WORKERS

Many people traditionally work at night—
bakers produce fresh bread for the morning,
and fishing crews bring their catch to shore
before sunrise. Astronomers stargaze in the
darkness, and doctors and nurses are ready
at any time of night to treat the sick. Some
tasks are easier when fewer people are up and
about—spare a thought for the workers who
clean, repair, and maintain our railroads, roads,
stores, and offices while we are tucked into bed.

Night flight

Long ago, when travelers used to rely on the stars and the moon to guide them on their way, journeys by night could often be a risky business. Today, all over the world, skilled pilots, flight attendants, and air-traffic controllers use sophisticated equipment to make sure that passengers on long flights are transported safely through the night skies.

Air-traffic controllers use radar to monitor aircraft. They give pilots permission to take off and land, and make sure that airplanes keep safe distances from each other.

At night aircraft marshals use illuminated wands to guide aircraft around the airport. Some airports, particularly those in built-up areas, restrict the number of airplanes that are allowed to take off and land during the night

As passengers on night flights are fast asleep, tucked under blankets, huge jet engines carry them through the darkness at speeds of up to 560 mph (900 km/h). In the cockpit the pilot and copilot are wide awake in front of hundreds of dials, instruments, switches, and levers that wink and shine in the darkness. The equipment shows exactly where the aircraft is, how fast it is going, how high it is flying, and how well the engines are running. From the nose of the airplane, radars scan the skies for other aircraft or for brewing storms. Screens in the cockpit display all the findings from the radars.

The onboard computer can take over to give the pilots a well-deserved break. In between takeoff and landing, the airplane can fly safely on autopilot for many thousands of miles.

During long night flights the team of attendants pull down the blinds and dim the main lights so that the passengers can relax and go to sleep. They also supply headphones so that people can listen to music or watch movies on TV screens. Passengers can also read under individual overhead lights. The flight attendants also serve snacks, meals, and drinks.

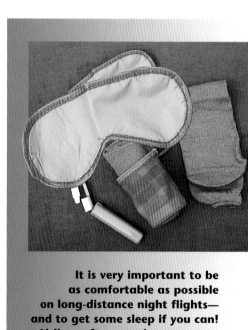

It is very important to be as comfortable as possible on long-distance night flights— and to get some sleep if you can! Airlines often supply passengers with packs that may include a comb, a toothbrush and toothpaste, an eye mask, socks or slippers, and a blanket.

Night nursing

Hospitals are staffed night and day,
365 days a year, ready to look after the sick.
Highly skilled doctors and nurses work hard,
handling emergencies and performing surgery,
as well as delivering babies, who make their
entrance no matter what time of night it is!

Hospitals do not stop during the night—they have to keep working like well-oiled machines. Teams of doctors, nurses, cleaners, receptionists, and volunteers keep things running smoothly and look after the people who stream into the hospital at all hours. The night shift starts work when the day teams go home.

Most operations are scheduled to take place during the day. However, some extremely complicated operations can last more than ten hours and continue into the night. Surgeons, nurses, and anesthetists work together to carry out the surgery. Operating rooms are sometimes also busy with emergencies.

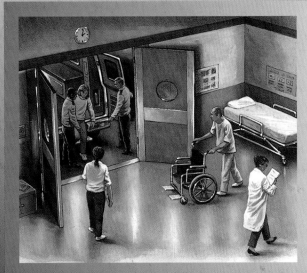

In the emergency room, or ER, the hospital staff need to be ready for any patients that the paramedics might bring to them in ambulances. The paramedics perform on-the-spot medical care at the scenes of an accident, but they must hurry to get the sick and injured to the hospital, where doctors can provide more extensive care with better equipment. The paramedics often radio the hospital as they speed through the night in the ambulances, so that the staff can make preparations for their arrival. The staff in the ER are always very busy, examining patients, referring patients to surgeons, and working hard to save lives.

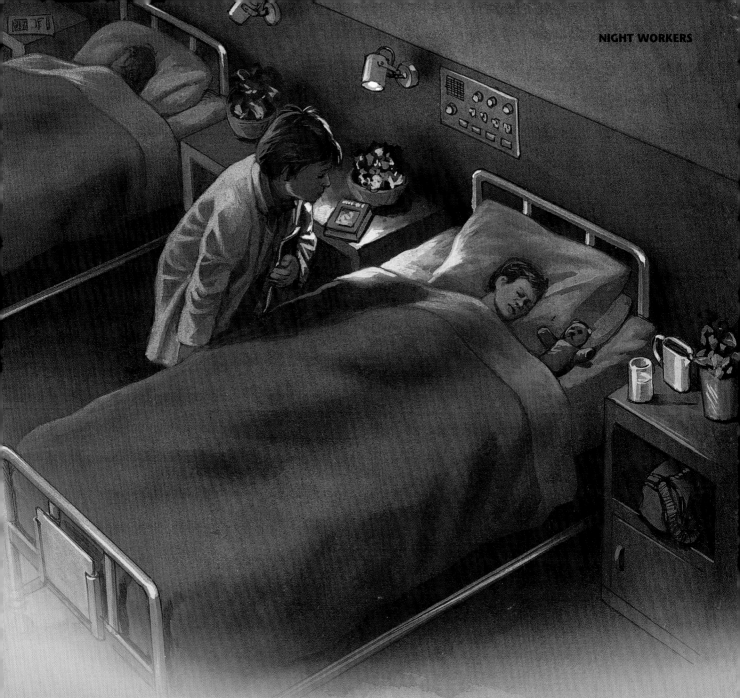

The hospital wards
are quieter during the night.
The outpatients, who do not stay the night, and all the
visitors have gone. The inpatients, asleep in their beds, are
watched over by night nurses. Specially trained nurses monitor
patients recovering from surgery in intensive care units. Every
night many doctors are on call—they can be called into action
at any time of the night to deal with emergencies or to check
patients in the wards. They try to grab a little sleep in small
hospital bedrooms in between duties.

The baker

Bakers work through the night so that fresh bread is ready for us each morning. Today most bread is baked in huge factories, but there are still some small bakeries that bake and sell delicious breads, cakes, and cookies.

Baking bread can be a tricky, lengthy task, and traditional bakers are very skilled. Early in the morning, long before the sun rises, bakers begin work in the small kitchens behind bakery shops.

Pressing and squeezing with their hands, they knead the dough—a mixture of flour, water, and yeast—and leave it to prove, or rise. They then cut and roll it into shape—sometimes creating complex swirls or braids. Then the dough is baked, often in wood-fired ovens. The bakers may also prepare cakes and pastries, which they display with the bread, fresh from the oven, in the shop windows.

Huge modern bakeries are equipped with all of the latest machines that carry out every stage of the bread-making process. Giant industrial mixers whirr and hum, preparing the dough; stainless steel traveling ovens roar like hungry furnaces, baking the thousands of identical loaves that pass through them on conveyor belts. Different machines then cool, slice, and wrap the loaves. The bread is loaded onto trucks and delivered to stores, ready for the morning. These factories work around the clock, seven days a week, and the night shift is the busiest time—12,000 loaves can be produced every hour. A team of people operates the machinery and makes sure everything runs smoothly.

Different types of bread

People in France go to bakeries, or Boulangeries, to buy bread called baguettes. These long, thin loaves are white and fluffy beneath a golden crust.

The dough of pita bread does not fully rise because it contains too little yeast. Mexican tortillas are unleavened flat breads—they contain no yeast at all.

Pumpernickel is a dark, slightly sour bread that comes from Germany. It is made with coarse rye flour and usually baked in long, square loaves.

Nightly news

We expect to be able to find out what is going on in the world at any time of day or night. A huge number of people work all night long, gathering and reporting news for television, radio, the internet, and newspapers.

There is no such thing as day or night at a live TV news channel—just one long, rolling broadcast that continues around the clock. Satellites beam live news and pictures all over the world so that millions of viewers can watch 24 hours a day.

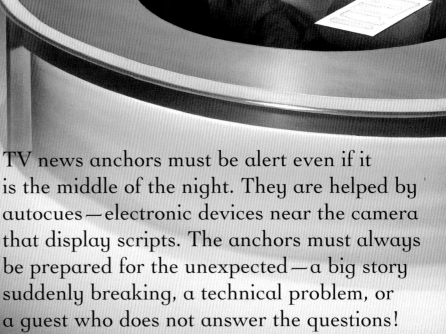

TV news anchors must be alert even if it is the middle of the night. They are helped by autocues—electronic devices near the camera that display scripts. The anchors must always be prepared for the unexpected—a big story suddenly breaking, a technical problem, or a guest who does not answer the questions!

The anchor and the rest of the studio team have to listen carefully to the director, who gives instructions from the control room during the program using a system called talkback.

Working hard behind the scenes, a team of researchers gathers information from special agencies and services to prepare news bulletins.

Reporters in hot spots all around the world keep in constant touch with newsrooms and deliver stories to them by satellite links.

The control room looks like the cockpit of a spaceship, full of switches, dials, buttons, and lights. From here the director monitors the studio on a bank of screens that show different camera angles. He or she can also view video recordings that need to be edited into programs and organize live interviews.

Journalists write at night so that the the latest news is in the morning paper. Only a few people operate printing presses, which print thousands of copies at a time.

Night fishing

The men and women who work on board night fishing boats do not have an easy job. In the darkness, as they haul up their heavy nets of fish, they battle against rough seas, stormy weather, and sometimes even sharks!

Fishing crews often need to travel far from land to find fish in the deep oceans, and their trips can last for several days. The crews trawl for fish all through the night to make the most of their time at sea. Every few hours they haul their nets out of the water, hoping for large catches. They empty the fish onto the decks and then lower the nets back into the dark ocean.

In between every haul of fish the crew has to try to get some food and sleep—no easy task if the boat is rolling from side to side on crashing waves! While some of the crew rest, the skipper must keep control of the boat from the wheelhouse.

Larger boats use sonar and computer systems to find big schools of fish. The crews of smaller boats, however, use more traditional methods. An experienced skipper can spot large schools shining in the moonlight near the surface of the water. Hungry seagulls or dolphins in search of fish suppers also guide the way— but the boats must hurry before the fish are eaten! If the crews are really lucky, the lights on their fishing boats will attract fish to them.

Once the fish have been caught, the crews pack them in ice to keep them fresh. Sometimes smaller boats deliver their catches to large factory ships that clean, gut, package, and freeze the fish, ready for delivery to stores.

Nets are not the only devices for catching fish. Explosives blast fish out of the water, and electric shocks stun them. In Asia some people train otters to do their fishing for them!

There are three kinds of nets used in the fishing industry.

Purse seines circle fish and then are pulled shut by lines that act like purse strings. They catch pelagic, or surface, fish such as tuna, salmon, and anchovies.

Trawl nets, or trawls, are funnel-shaped nets that are dragged along the seabed to catch demersal, or deep-sea fish, such as cod, sole, and haddock.

Gill nets trap fish by their gills. Some gill nets used to drift along and catch every type of sea life. These drift nets, known as walls of death, are now banned.

The astronomer

Throughout history, people have gazed into space in awe. The ancient Greeks were the first astronomers to list all the stars they could see with the naked eye. Today professional astronomers use powerful telescopes and modern technology to discover what is really out there.

Telescopes work best at night because there is no light from the sun, and objects in space stand out clearly against the dark sky. Astronomers often work late into the night to get the best views of space.

Astronomers are skilled scientists, technicians, and engineers who work together to collect and analyze electronic information from telescopes. Telescopes act as giant cameras that take pictures of space, but it is possible to look through them directly. Professional astronomers from all over the world travel to large observatories to spend a few precious nights observing stars and galaxies that are millions of light-years away.

Telescopes are housed in observatories, which are usually
built in remote places, far from the light pollution caused
by the bright lights from cities. The best locations are
deserts, where the night skies are clear and cloudless,
or mountaintops above the clouds and city smog.

Mauna Kea, a dormant volcano in Hawaii, is home to
many observatories that dot the barren landscape with
their space-age domes. The eight-story-high domes
protect the telescopes from wind and
rain. All day, air conditioners
keep the temperature
inside the domes near
freezing so that
when the roofs
open at night, the
telescopes are not
affected by the
cold night air.

NIGHT SKY

When you look up at the sky on a clear,
cloudless night, thousands of stars shine
and twinkle in the velvety darkness. Their
light has traveled billions of miles through
space. Much nearer you'll see the moon,
our closest neighbor, and you may even
see a planet, shining steadily. They are
all part of our galaxy, the Milky Way,
which even without a telescope can
be a spectacular sight.

Night and day

We know that darkness falls and temperatures drop during the night, but why does this happen? To find the answer, we must look at the bigger picture out in space and discover how night is caused by the movements of our planet, Earth, and its star, the sun. Occasionally the moon also plays a part, turning day into night as it eclipses the sun.

As Earth orbits the sun in huge loops it spins on its axis, an imaginary line running through its center from the North Pole to the South Pole. It takes 24 hours to complete one spin. As Earth revolves the part of it that faces the sun, receiving its light and warmth, experiences day. The rest of the planet is plunged into the darkness of night. When it is day in Africa, on the other side of the globe in North America it is night.

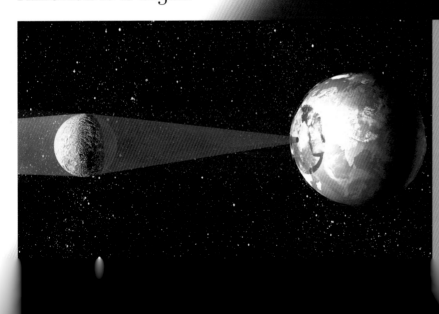

Day becomes night during an eclipse of the sun, or solar eclipse. When the moon, which orbits Earth, moves in between Earth and the sun, it casts a shadow onto Earth. The small area that lies directly in the moon's shadow experiences a total eclipse. A larger, partly shadowed area experiences a partial eclipse. The sun is about 400 times larger than the moon, but the moon is about 400 times closer to Earth than the sun, so during a total eclipse, the moon appears to completely cover the sun.

The length of night and day varies because Earth's axis tilts, and as it completes its orbit of the sun different parts of the planet are tipped toward the sun at different times of the year. From May to August the Northern Hemisphere is tipped toward the sun, so it experiences summer. This means that as Earth spins around, light from the sun hits the Northern Hemisphere for longer each day, causing longer days and shorter nights. During the same months the Southern Hemisphere is tilted away from the sun and receives less sunlight. It experiences winter, with shorter days and longer nights. Areas near the equator face the sun at all times of the year. This means that they do not have any seasons, and the days and nights are always about the same length.

The moon

The moon is the biggest and brightest object in our night sky. Although it seems to glow, it has no light of its own, but rather reflects light from the sun. It appears so large because it is close to us in space. It is really much smaller than the stars, which look so tiny.

It is not difficult to understand why the moon, with its beautiful pale light, was worshiped in ancient times. In Greece the moon was represented by the goddess Selene, who drove a chariot across the night sky. In ancient Egypt the moon god Thoth was worshiped. He had a human body and the head of an ibis—a wading bird.

During its cycles the moon waxes and wanes, or grows and shrinks, changing from a tiny, silver sliver into a large, shining globe and back again. Long ago some people believed that a full moon could cause insanity. The word "lunatic," meaning insane, comes from the Latin word *luna*, which means moon.

The moon appears to change shape as different parts of it reflect the sun's light during its orbit around Earth. The different shapes are known as the phases of the moon.

NEW MOON

WAXING CRESCENT

FIRST QUARTER

WAXING GIBBOUS

Different kinds of craters on the moon's surface

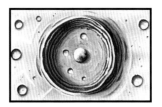

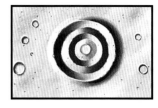

A terraced crater has sides like huge, steep steps and mountains in its center.

A concentric crater looks like a series of smaller rings inside larger rings.

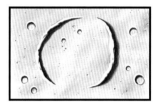

A ray crater has streaks, or rays, of light-colored rocks surrounding it.

A ghost crater is an old crater almost totally filled in by molten rock.

A moon is a rocky object that orbits a planet. Our moon is about four billion years old. As it orbits Earth it spins on its axis, keeping the same side facing toward Earth. On this side we can see both light and dark patches. The light patches are mountains, valleys, and craters. The craters, some more than 124 miles (200km) wide, were formed by asteroids crashing into the moon's surface. The dark patches are vast plains created by molten rock. They are known as *maria*, the Latin for seas, but they do not contain water. The Sea of Tranquility and the Ocean of Storms are *maria* on the moon.

FULL MOON **WANING GIBBOUS** **LAST QUARTER** **WANING CRESCENT** **OLD MOON**

81

Eclipse of the moon

**Every so often we are treated to a
very special nighttime performance
when the moon darkens and turns
a magnificent, coppery red color.
This strange sight is caused
by an eclipse of the moon.**

When Earth eclipses, or casts
its shadow over, the moon,
it is known as an eclipse of the
moon, or a lunar eclipse. This
occurs when the moon is on the
opposite side of Earth to the
sun. Because Earth lies directly
between the sun and the moon,
it blocks the light to the moon
and casts its dark shadow over it.

The moon normally glows brightly
because it reflects light from the sun.
When the moon is eclipsed it receives
no light directly from the sun, so it
appears darker. The moon does not
completely disappear from sight during
a lunar eclipse, but it glows an orange-red.
This is because a small amount of light from the
sun is able to filter through Earth's atmosphere into
Earth's shadow to bathe the moon in a coppery glow.

Throughout history people have watched eclipses, both lunar and solar, with fear and fascination, amazed by unusual events that many believed were the work of gods.

In 1504 Christopher Columbus, the famous Italian explorer, took advantage of such beliefs. When he was marooned on the island of Jamaica, the local people refused to give him food. Columbus knew that a lunar eclipse was predicted for February 29, so he arranged a meeting with the people on that night. Columbus told them that God was so angry with them, He was going to take the moon away. When the eclipse happened right on cue the people were so frightened that they gave food to Columbus immediately!

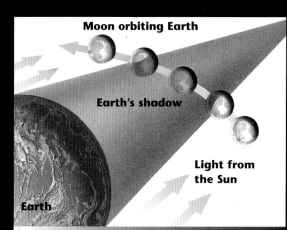

Moon orbiting Earth

Earth's shadow

Light from the Sun

Earth

No special equipment is needed to observe lunar eclipses—there is no bright sunlight to damage your eyes—but a pair of binoculars or a small telescope will help you get a closer look. Then all you need to do is hope for clear skies, and enjoy the show.

When all of the moon is completely covered by Earth's shadow, people on the part of Earth that faces the moon will see a total lunar eclipse. When the moon is only partly shadowed during its orbit, a partial lunar eclipse will be seen. The moon orbits Earth about every 27 days, but lunar eclipses occur only up to three times a year. This is because the moon does not pass through Earth's shadow every time it orbits Earth.

Men on the moon

Over the years, there have been many fascinating stories about the moon. An early science fiction story described a moon that was inhabited by fleas twelve times the size of elephants! Today we no longer have to invent stories about the moon—on July 20, 1969, two men actually walked on its surface.

American astronauts Neil Armstrong and Edwin "Buzz" Aldrin touched down on the moon's surface in their lunar module, the *Eagle*, as part of NASA's Apollo 11 mission in 1969. Armstrong famously declared, "The Eagle has landed."

As commander of the mission, Armstrong was the first to step out of the *Eagle*, and in doing so he made history, becoming the first human to set foot on the moon. Followed closely by Aldrin, Armstrong set up a TV camera so that the world could watch live the astronauts' first weightless steps. The two astronauts left behind a plaque.

> **Here men from planet Earth first set foot upon the moon, July 1969. We came in peace for all mankind.**

Armstrong and Aldrin carried out experiments, collecting soil samples and taking photographs. Since their historic landing, there have been five more Apollo missions to the moon. We now know that the moon is a dry, dead world with no air, wind or weather, and definitely no giant fleas!

The planets

Nine planets, including Earth, orbit the sun as part of our solar system. The six planets closest to Earth— Mercury, Venus, Mars, Jupiter, Saturn, and Uranus—are just visible to the naked eye in some parts of Earth's night sky.

MERCURY is hard to see from Earth because it is so close to the sun's glare. It orbits the sun faster than all the other planets, taking just 88 days.

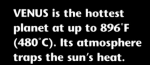

VENUS is the hottest planet at up to 896°F (480°C). Its atmosphere traps the sun's heat.

EARTH looks blue from space because two thirds of its surface is covered by ocean. Formed about 4.6 billion years ago, its atmosphere contains a lot of oxygen, which makes life possible.

MARS is known as the Red Planet because iron-rich dust has turned its surface and sky red. Scientists believe that life in the form of bacteria could exist on Mars because space probes that have landed on the planet discovered that water once existed there.

The SUN, a huge ball of hot gas, is our nearest star, and it is so large that more than one million Earths would fit inside it. Its size creates a large gravitational pull that keeps the nine planets spinning around it in orbit.

JUPITER is the fifth planet from the sun, and unlike the four planets closest to the Sun, which are small, rocky bodies, it is a huge ball of gas with no solid surface. The largest planet in our solar system, Jupiter spins on its axis very quickly, creating stripes and whirlpools of gas on its surface.

URANUS is only just visible from Earth with the naked eye. It was discovered with a telescope in 1781 by English astronomer William Herschel. Uranus spins on an axis that, unlike the axes of most planets, is almost horizontal. This explains why it is nicknamed the topsy-turvy planet.

SATURN, like Jupiter, Uranus, and Neptune, is made of gas. Bright yellow in color, it is surrounded by huge, shining rings made of millions of pieces of ice and rocks that whizz around the planet. Saturn is the lightest planet—if it were dropped into a huge bowl of water, it would float!

PLUTO, a ball of icy rock, is the smallest and coldest planet. It is so far away from the sun that it takes 248 Earth years to orbit it. Even with the most powerful telescope Pluto appears as a faint dot.

NEPTUNE is bright blue because its atmosphere contains methane gas. Neptune is not visible to the naked eye and was discovered only when astronomers in the 1800s realized that the orbit of Uranus was being affected by the gravity of a large body—Neptune.

The universe

The moon, stars, and planets are all part of our galaxy, the Milky Way— a huge spiraling collection of glittering stars, moons, and planets. With the aid of powerful telescopes we can look at beautiful and amazing things in other parts of the universe.

Galaxy NGC 4603 is a spiral galaxy, like the Milky Way. The arms of this galaxy are made of young, bright-blue stars and red giant stars. A red giant is a huge red star that has expanded greatly and is near the end of its life.

Andromeda, another spiral galaxy, is the nearest major galaxy to us in the universe. It is 2.2 million light-years away, but amazingly it is visible in our night sky. It is the most distant object that we can see without a telescope.

A supernova is a huge star that collapses and then is torn apart in an explosion brighter than billions of our suns put together. On telescope images a supernova appears as a small but bright flash of color, surrounded by rings of debris.

The universe is everything that exists anywhere— all solid, liquid, and gaseous matter. It is too vast to imagine, and when we study the night sky, even with powerful telescopes we can see only a tiny fraction of it. The universe contains billions of galaxies, which themselves contain billions of stars, gas, and dust particles that stay together because of their gravitational pull.

Our galaxy, the Milky Way, is a spiral galaxy—it has a central bulge with several arms spiraling around it. The sun, our nearest star, lies in an arm of the Milky Way called the Orion Arm. Distances in the universe are so vast that we measure them in light-years. The Milky Way is about 100,000 light-years across—light takes about 100,000 years to travel across the galaxy.

A nebula is a vast cloud of dust and gas. Many nebulae are "nurseries" where new stars are born. At the heart of some nebulae fiercely hot stars heat the gas, making it glow beautifully like a huge cavern lit with colorful lanterns.

Butterfly nebulae are also known as twin-jet nebulae. If the nebula is sliced in half, it looks like the two exhausts of a jet engine. The nebula's gas travels at more than 186 miles (300km) per second—like a very powerful jet engine.

Some of the stars that we see shining like pinpoints in our night sky are about 1,000 light-years away. When we see these stars, we are seeing light that has taken 1,000 years to reach us, so we are seeing the stars as they looked 1,000 years ago. By the time their light reaches us, the stars that we see may have changed, exploded, or even disappeared without us ever knowing.

The International Space Station, or ISS, orbits Earth. It may be finished as early as 2004. Huge solar panels, or arrays, absorb heat from the sun to power the station. The arrays reflect the sun's light, making ISS visible to the naked eye at night.

Natural fireworks

A comet streaking through the inky night sky, its tail trailing behind it for millions of miles, is one of the most spectacular sights to be seen from Earth.

Thousands of years ago, a comet would have filled the hearts of our ancestors with fear and dread. They believed that comets were omens of doom that caused death, disaster, war, and plague in their wake. Today we know that comets are lumps of ice and rock traveling in huge, looping orbits around the sun. There are a vast number of comets in the outer regions of our solar system.

Meteors, or shooting stars, the tiny grains of dust left behind by comets as they swoop past the sun, can be seen burning up in the atmosphere on most nights of the year. But at certain times there are meteor showers, when you can see as many as 60 meteors in an hour. This happens when Earth travels through huge clouds of comet debris, and the meteor showers light up the sky like natural firework displays. Keep an eye out for the Perseids around August 12 and the Geminids just before the middle of December.

A comet's tail can be millions of miles in length.

The beautiful Northern and Southern Lights—
the Aurora Borealis and the Aurora Australis—
are dazzling natural light shows. They take place
around the North and South poles, respectively,
and occur when electrically charged particles from
the sun are drawn into Earth's magnetic field. The
glowing curtain of red and green light that we see
is the result of these particles slamming into the
uppermost fringes of our atmosphere.

A comet's orbit leads
it on a regular flying visit close
to the sun from the farthest reaches of our
solar system. As it gets nearer to the sun, it starts to
evaporate in the heat and grows a gigantic tail of gas and dust.

Halley's Comet, last visible from Earth between 1985 and 1986,
is named after the English scientist Edmond Halley. He was the first
to suggest that comets orbit the sun. He spotted this particular comet
in 1682, and calculated that it would pass by Earth every 76 years.
Comet Hale-Bopp was one of the brightest comets of the 1900s. It
was visible to the naked eye for 19 months during 1996 and 1997.

Constellations
in the Northern
Hemisphere's sky

1. PEGASUS

Pegasus, an immortal
winged horse, was one
of 48 constellations
named in A.D. 150 by
the Greek astronomer
Ptolemy.

2. HERCULES

Hercules is another
figure from Greek
mythology. He was
famous for his
immense strength
and some say size.

3. URSA MAJOR

Ursa Major, the Great
Bear, is not too hard
to see. The seven stars
in its tail and lower
back are known as
the Big Dipper.

4. LEO

Leo, the lion, is one
of the 12 signs of
the zodiac. It is one
of the few patterns
that resembles what
it is supposed to be!

Look to the stars

For thousands of years people have looked
up at the stars and tried to make sense of them.
Ancient astronomers imagined that the patterns
of shining stars were gods and goddesses, birds,
animals, and fish. These star patterns belong to
sections of the sky we now call constellations.

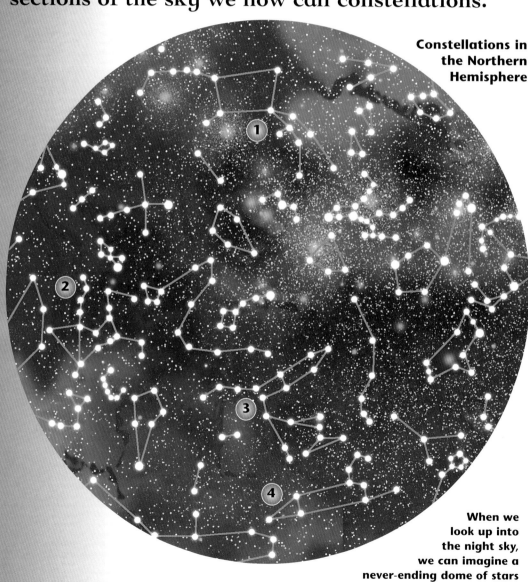

**Constellations in
the Northern
Hemisphere**

When we
look up into
the night sky,
we can imagine a
never-ending dome of stars
that surrounds us. This is known as the
celestial sphere. The sphere is divided into
a northern and southern hemisphere—just
like Earth. The stars in each hemisphere
can be mapped onto two flat circles.

More than 3,000 years ago astronomers in the city of Babylon made rough maps of the patterns that the brightest stars made. They also observed the sun, the moon, and the planets as they moved across a narrow band of stars. They came to the conclusion that this band of stars had an important effect on the lives of people on Earth, and they divided the band into 12 constellations. Each constellation of stars represents a sign of the zodiac. Today astrologers use the zodiac to try to predict the future.

Constellations in the Southern Hemisphere's sky

5. PHOENIX

The Phoenix is the firebird from ancient Arabian mythology. Every 500 years it set fire to itself and rose again from the ashes.

6. SCORPIO

Scorpio, the scorpion, is another sign of the zodiac. Its brightest star, Antares, is 10,000 times more luminous than our sun.

7. LIBRA

Libra, known as the scales, is a small and faint constellation. It is the seventh sign of the zodiac.

8. CRUX

Crux, the Southern Cross, is the smallest constellation of both hemispheres. Crux is a Latin word that means cross.

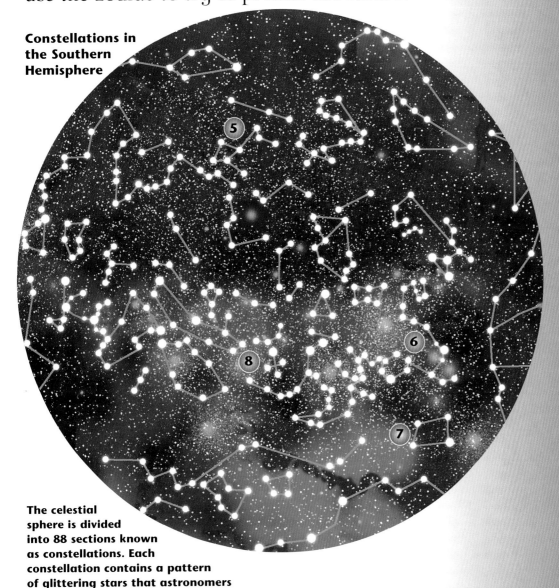

Constellations in the Southern Hemisphere

The celestial sphere is divided into 88 sections known as constellations. Each constellation contains a pattern of glittering stars that astronomers have named over the years. Constellations in the southern celestial sphere can only be seen from Earth's Southern Hemisphere—the Southern Cross cannot be seen in the Northern Hemisphere.

NEW DAWN

As dawn breaks the sun creeps above the horizon, slowly stealing the scene from the night with its pale and brilliant glow. The last traces of nighttime magic and mystery vanish with the darkness—until next time. . . .

INDEX